All the material in this book was confirmed as accurate at the time of publication.

In memory of Beefsteak Charlie's, where long ago
I waited tables on K street in Washington, D.C. —J.P.

To everyone who supported me in all shapes and forms. You know who you are. —S.A.

Text © 2025 James Preller. Illustrations © 2025 Sonya Abby

First published in 2025 by Wide Eyed Editions, an imprint of The Quarto Group.
100 Cummings Center, Suite 265D, Beverly, MA 01915, USA.
T +1 978-282-9590 www.Quarto.com

ISBN 978-1-83600-131-7
eBook ISBN 978-1-83600-132-4

The illustrations were created digitally
Set in Quicksand and Thirsty Script

Designer: Vanessa Lovegrove
Editor: Leah Baxter
Production Controller: Dawn Cameron
Art Director: Karissa Santos
Publisher: Debbie Foy

Manufactured in Guangdong, China TT122024

9 8 7 6 5 4 3 2 1

Only in Washington, D.C.

Written by **James Preller** · Illustrated by **Sonya Abby**

WIDE EYED EDITIONS

Contents

MARYLAND

POTOMAC RIVER

The city of Washington is the capital of the United States—but it is not part of a state. It is a separate district called the DISTRICT OF COLUMBIA, consisting of land borrowed from neighboring states, Maryland and Virginia.

Washington, D.C., is truly an INTERNATIONAL city, home to more than 170 embassies and cultural centers. People from all over the world come to visit, work and live here, and more than 25 percent of the city's residents speak a language other than English in their homes.

Welcome to Washington, D.C.

Are you buckled up and ready to roll? Have you got your toothbrush and a snack for the journey? Great, because we are going on a wild, wonderful, and sometimes wacky trip to Washington, D.C. We'll visit famous places, moving memorials, cool neighborhoods, and many of the world's most amazing museums. Where else can you sit on Albert Einstein's lap, paddleboard past Thomas Jefferson, or marvel at a *Star Wars* Starfighter? There's something for everyone in this wonderful city! Keep an eye out for some of the offbeat, unusual, and just-plain-weird attractions, festivals, history, landmarks, and people that make this capital city unlike anywhere else on the planet.

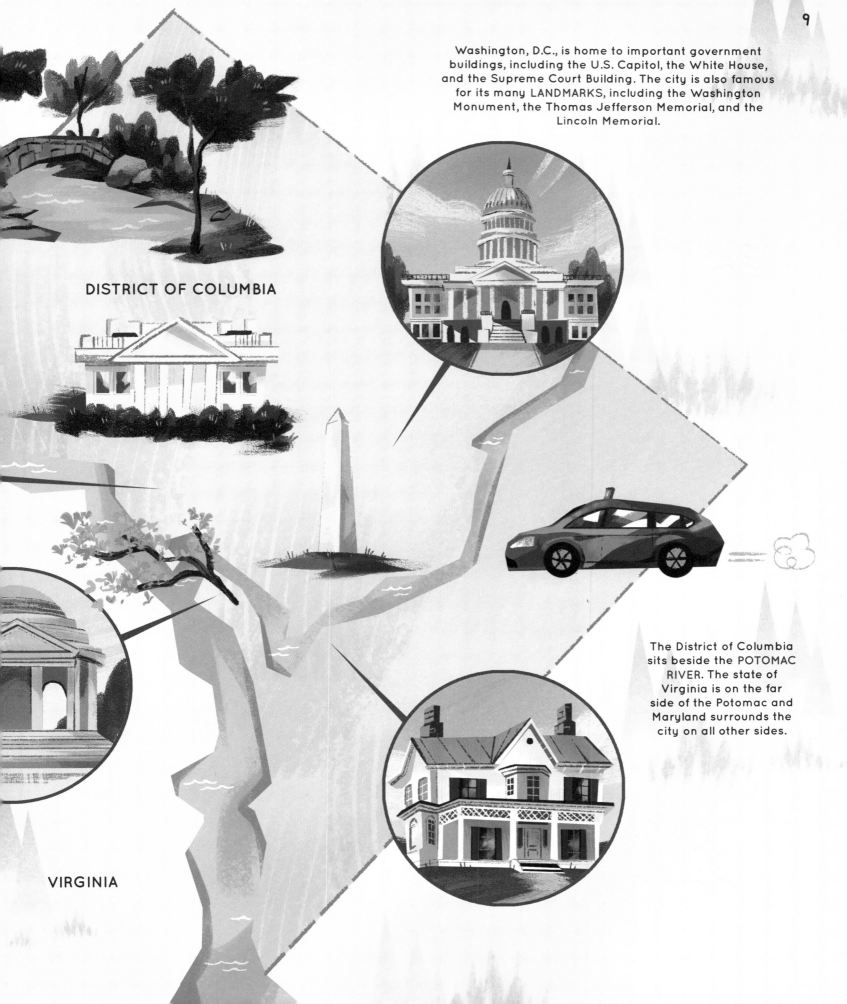

Washington, D.C., is home to important government buildings, including the U.S. Capitol, the White House, and the Supreme Court Building. The city is also famous for its many LANDMARKS, including the Washington Monument, the Thomas Jefferson Memorial, and the Lincoln Memorial.

DISTRICT OF COLUMBIA

The District of Columbia sits beside the POTOMAC RIVER. The state of Virginia is on the far side of the Potomac and Maryland surrounds the city on all other sides.

VIRGINIA

The White House

The White House is one of the most famous buildings in the world. It is, after all, where the president of the United States lives and works. No visit to Washington, D.C., would be complete without spending at least a few minutes outside the gates of 1600 Pennsylvania Avenue. If you are lucky, you might even take a tour! Over the years, the White House has been burned down, rebuilt, expanded, torn down, and repaired again. It stands as a symbol of America, and like the country, it continues to change with the times.

The US government was originally based in Philadelphia, Pennsylvania. But in 1791, George Washington selected a new, permanent site for the White House. It wasn't ready for its first occupants, President JOHN AND ABIGAIL ADAMS, until 1800, one year after Washington died. Today, every U.S. president except Washington has called the White House home.

The White House has 35 bathrooms, 8 staircases, 147 windows, 28 fireplaces, 12 chimneys, 412 doors, 132 rooms— and a ghost, maybe. British Prime Minister Winston Churchill claimed to have seen LINCOLN'S GHOST during a visit!

According to the White House Historical Association, the city commissioners enlisted the labor of enslaved BLACK AMERICANS to help build the White House and other government buildings. They worked as brickmakers, carpenters, and quarrymen.

The White House has a swimming pool, billiard room, putting green, bowling lane and jogging track. In 2009, President BARACK OBAMA updated the basketball and tennis courts. Swish!

Is the president home? Just look for the AMERICAN FLAG. If it's flying on the flagpole, that means the president is in town.

Washington, D.C. has long been a site for demonstrations, marches, vigils, and protests. The first picketers at the White House were the SUFFRAGISTS. Their protests began in 1917 and helped lead to the passing of the 19th Amendment in 1920, granting women the right to vote.

Do you know who never slept a single night in LINCOLN'S BEDROOM? Old Honest Abe himself! Lincoln used that space for cabinet meetings.

What's a POTUS, you might ask? It's a fast, easy abbreviation for President of the United States. Just mash the first letters of each word together!

By 1948, the White House had become run-down and unsafe. So President HARRY S. TRUMAN moved out to a hotel across the street! He didn't move back in until repairs were completed in 1952.

During the WAR OF 1812, rowdy British troops set the White House on fire. In 1929 on Christmas Eve, a blocked chimney caused a fire, nearly destroying the West Wing.

Did you know that the OVAL OFFICE is actually a trapezoid? You didn't? Well, that's good—because it's not! It's oval-shaped. Thus, the name. The office was built during President Howard Taft's administration, in 1909.

Stats & Facts

FAST FACTS

ABBREVIATION: D.C.
DATE FOUNDED: July 16, 1790
POPULATION: Around 680,000
AREA: 68.34 square miles

The DISTINCTIVE FLAG of Washington, D.C. was adopted in 1938. The flag was designed by Charles A. R. Dunn, based on the coat of arms used by George Washington's family.

D.C. SUPERLATIVES

- At 409 feet, Fort Reno Park is the HIGHEST POINT in Washington, D.C.
- The LOWEST POINT in the city is at sea level, at the Potomac River.
- The HOTTEST DAY ever recorded in the city, July 20, 1930, saw temperatures reach 106°F.
- February 11, 1899 was the COLDEST DAY ever recorded, with lows of -15°F
- At just over 555 feet, the Washington Monument is the world's TALLEST OBELISK.

Next-Door Neighbors

NORTH: Maryland   WEST: Virginia

WHAT'S IN A NAME?

The city's name, Washington, D.C., was inspired by—you guessed it!—the nation's first president, GEORGE WASHINGTON. "D.C." stands for the District of Columbia, named after the navigator Christopher Columbus, whose journeys to the Americas in the late 1400s began a period of European colonization, with devastating results for the Indigenous peoples.

The District's official MOTTO is Justitia Omnibus—Latin for "Justice for all."

On January 28, 1898, construction workers found fossilized remains of a dinosaur that had lived 100 million years ago. In 1990, paleontologist Peter Krantz informally named it "Capitalsaurus" and the name caught on. It's the OFFICIAL DINOSAUR of the city and January 28 is now "Capitalsaurus Day."

Washington, D.C. has long been known as "Our Nation's Capital." Today, most locals refer to it as "THE DISTRICT" or simply, "D.C."

SOUTH: Maryland   EAST: Maryland

The National Mall

The National Mall is an inspiring two-mile strip of land that stretches from the Capitol Building to the Lincoln Memorial. Think of it as the nation's front yard! Go for a wander and you'll discover monuments, museums, and memorials every step of the way. The Mall tells a moving story about the history of America and the many moments of sacrifice that have helped to define the nation, so soak it all up and give yourself time to pause and reflect.

The Mall is home to many IMPRESSIVE MUSEUMS, most notably the United States Holocaust Memorial Museum, the National Gallery of Art, the National Museum of the American Indian, and the National Museum of African Art. For these pages we'll explorethe outdoor areas of the Mall, but check out pages 40–41 for a closer look at some of Washington D.C.'s museum highlights.

The CHERRY TREES that line the Mall were a gift from Japan in 1912. They are an enduring reminder of the friendship between the two countries. The cherry tree is said to bring good fortune and happiness.

It was here that Martin Luther King, Jr. delivered his famous "I HAVE A DREAM" speech to 250,000 people gathered before the Lincoln Memorial. He told the crowd, "Now is the time to lift our nation from the quicksands of racial injustice to the solid rock of brotherhood." An etching marks the spot where he stood on that day in 1963.

Take a look at the 555-foot column that is the WASHINGTON MONUMENT. It was constructed from more than 36,000 pieces of marble and granite, and the fifty flags surrounding it each represent a state. The monument, or obelisk, is the tallest freestanding stone structure in the world!

The Mural Wall of the KOREAN WAR VETERANS MEMORIAL includes more than 2,400 photographs of men, women, and even a dog who served in the Korean War.

There are few sights as awesome as the 19-foot marble statue of Abraham Lincoln, the president who fought to end slavery, seated inside the LINCOLN MEMORIAL. The surrounding walls are engraved with the great words he spoke.

The REFLECTING POOL is one of the most-photographed sights in Washington, D.C. It is especially magical at night, when the shimmering lights sparkle on the water.

The VIETNAM VETERANS MEMORIAL is profound in its simplicity. It is a black wall inscribed with the names of all 58,318 Americans who lost their lives in the Vietnam War.

Dedicated in 2011, the MARTIN LUTHER KING, JR. MEMORIAL was the Mall's first memorial to an African American. It was created by Chinese sculptor Lei Yixin.

History Timeline

Over 4,000 years ago
The Nacotchtank (also known as Anacostan) and Piscataway peoples inhabit the future site of the District of Columbia.

1608 Led by Captain John Smith, English explorers sail up the Potomac River, becoming the first colonizers to set eyes on the Nacotchtank village.

1619 English colonialists bring enslaved people from Africa (present-day Angola) to Virginia, where they are traded in exchange for supplies, beginning what will become the institution of slavery in America. Tobacco fields are established, with enslaved people being forced to work on them.

1862 The District of Columbia Compensated Emancipation Act frees more than 3,000 enslaved people in Washington, D.C. alone.

1861 The Civil War begins, with Washington, D.C. becoming the military headquarters of the Union Army.

1865 Just days after the end of the Civil War, President Abraham Lincoln is assassinated by John Wilkes Booth, a Confederate sympathizer, at Ford's Theatre in D.C.

1867 Howard University becomes the nation's first Black University, with the goal of providing more opportunities for Black Americans in a post-slavery United States.

1870s The population of Washington, D.C. grows significantly after the conclusion of the Civil War. Many newly freed people move to the city.

1884 After a long delay, the Washington Monument is completed. The obelisk stands at just over 555 feet, making it the tallest human-made structure in the world at that time.

1888 The first electrified streetcars appear in the city.

1968 Martin Luther King, Jr. is assassinated in Memphis, Tennessee. In response, riots break out in Washington, D.C. and across the nation.

1963 Martin Luther King, Jr. delivers the "I Have a Dream" speech on the steps of the Lincoln Memorial.

1961 The 23rd Amendment allows Washington, D.C. residents to vote in presidential elections for the first time. Up to that point, because of D.C.'s unique status as a district, local citizens did not have the same voting rights as citizens of the 50 states.

1972 On loan from China, Hsing-Hsing and Ling-Ling, a pair of giant pandas, move into the National Zoo and become overnight sensations.

1976 The Metro begins operating, connecting diverse parts of the city and neighboring suburbs.

1977 Washington, D.C.'s Human Rights Act is one of the first laws in the country designed to protect gay and lesbian people from discrimination.

1984 The Georgetown Hoyas win the NCAA (National Collegiate Athletics Association) Basketball Championship.

1663–1700 Lord Baltimore, an English colonizer, grants Nacotchtank lands to European settlers. Nacotchtank fight a losing battle against sickness and violent displacement and, by the turn of the century, they have been driven from their land.

1776 The United States Declaration of Independence is signed.

1790 Washington, D.C. is founded.

1800 The nation's capital is moved from Philadelphia to Washington, D.C.

1814 Invading British troops burn large parts of Washington, D.C., including the White House and the U.S. Capitol.

1850 Congress abolishes the trade of enslaved African people in the District of Columbia.

1848 Building of the Washington Monument begins.

1846 Congress establishes the Smithsonian, dedicated to the "increase and diffusion" of knowledge. Today, it is the largest museum and research complex in the world.

1890 Rock Creek Park is established.

1909 As a gift of friendship, the Mayor of Tokyo presents the city with 2,000 cherry trees.

1910 The first automobiles begin to appear on the city's streets.

1924 The Washington Senators baseball team wins the World Series.

1954 Segregation in playgrounds is ended in the District of Columbia. That same year, the Supreme Court rules that segregation in the city's schools is unconstitutional.

1953 Yankee slugger Mickey Mantle hits a legendary 565-foot home run in Griffith Stadium.

1953 In a landmark court case, the Supreme Court rules that segregation policies at Thompson's cafeteria are illegal, marking a huge step forward for the Black community and the fight to end segregation.

1939 Marian Anderson sings before 75,000 people at the Lincoln Memorial in a stand against racial inequality.

1991 Eleanor Holmes Norton, from the District of Columbia, becomes delegate to the U.S. House of Representatives. A lifelong activist, she remains the District's fiercest advocate for universal human and civil rights.

2016 The National Museum of African American History and Culture opens on the National Mall.

2018 The Washington Capitals hockey team wins their first Stanley Cup.

2021 Supporters of President Donald Trump violently storm the U.S. Capitol as members of Congress meet to certify the results of the 2020 presidential election.

The National Museum of Natural History

The National Museum of Natural History delights and inspires visitors looking to learn about the natural world. With millions of amazing artifacts, each one tells a story about the beautiful planet that we call home. Under one roof, you can investigate insects and visit a butterfly pavilion, meet the fossils of countless intriguing sea creatures, or step back in time to marvel at the only Neanderthal skeleton on display in North America.

Don't miss the giant replica of the AEDES MOSQUITO. But don't worry, it hasn't buzzed its way down to suck anyone's blood just yet.

The museum is home to the oldest continuously operating INSECT ZOO in the country, which opened in 1976. You can get up close and personal with the bugs, and sometimes even watch live tarantula feedings—just make sure you're not on the menu!

Lions and tigers and bears, oh my! You must have found your way to the MAMMALS EXHIBIT. If you're feeling brave enough, stay for a while to learn all about our very own family tree.

Ever wanted to learn more about your ancestors? Check out the five bronze statues of EARLY HOMINIDS (the group of primates that includes modern-day humans) that lived from 2.5 million years ago to roughly 40,000 years ago.

GINGER BEAR

Among the museum's many weird and wonderful specimens is the PINK FAIRY ARMADILLO. The creature is so small it would fit in the palm of your hand.

No matter how much you like eggs for your breakfast, we don't recommend messing with the ALLOSAURUS SKELETON that can be found guarding its eggs in the Hall of Fossils. Maybe, just for today, eat a muffin instead.

From emeralds and rubies to meteorites and volcanic lava, get to know your ROCKS AND MINERALS in the Gem and Mineral Hall. Don't miss the super-famous, super-sparkly, Hope Diamond—the largest deep-blue diamond ever found.

BUTTERFLIES are free to flutter about in the wonderful Butterfly Pavilion, landing on plants and sometimes people!

Have you ever wondered how big a T. REX really is? Well you're in luck, because you can see a complete T-rex fossil on display at the museum. You can also see the skeletons of a Triceratops and a Megacerops.

Say hello to Henry! Wait, who's Henry? Henry is the 13-foot-tall, 11-ton AFRICAN BUSH ELEPHANT that lives in the museum entrance hall. He's pretty hard to miss and has been welcoming visitors since 1959.

Spectacular Sports

Make no mistake, Washington, D.C. is a sporting hot spot! The city is a great place for outdoor adventures, from golf to tennis, and paddleboarding to cycling. But if you'd rather sit and watch while others do all the work, Washington, D.C. also offers a huge range of elite professional sports—there's no better place to catch a game!

Washington, D.C. is home to teams from seven of the BIGGEST PROFESSIONAL SPORTS LEAGUES. How many of the teams can you name? See the last page of this book for a list.

PAX THE PANDA is the official mascot for the Mystics. Pax loves bamboo and basketball!

The rising stars of women's basketball take to the court for WASHINGTON MYSTICS games at the Entertainment and Sports Arena. In the Mystics' first season in 1998, they won only three games for a 3-27 record. But by 2019, they were WNBA Champs!

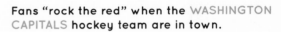

Fans "rock the red" when the WASHINGTON CAPITALS hockey team are in town.

The PRESIDENTS RACE takes place during every Washington Nationals home game at Nationals Park. Four presidential team mascots—Teddy, Abe, George, and Tom—are cheered on by the crowd as they bumble, bump, jostle, and sprint their way to the finish line.

The beautiful NATIONALS PARK BASEBALL STADIUM, which opened in 2008 and is home to the Washington Nationals, helped revitalize the entire Capital Riverfront area. The park offers magnificent views of the Capitol and the Washington Monument.

SOCCER FANS can enjoy both men's and women's leagues, with D.C. United (from Major League Soccer) and Washington Spirit (featuring stars of the National Women's Soccer League) both based in the city. The two teams share the stadium at Audi Field—but not at the same time!

KAYAKERS love dipping their paddles in the Chesapeake and Ohio Canal in Georgetown, or floating through the Potomac River's Tidal Basin to the Jefferson Memorial.

Hi!

Chesapeake Bay is one of the best spots for SAILING in the world.

D.C. local James Bradford made it big in the WORLD OF WEIGHTLIFTING. Very big in fact. Bradford won silver medals in two Olympics, 1952 and 1960.

Visitors might see a lot of burgundy and gold during football season. That's how the city's enthusiastic football fans show support for their beloved WASHINGTON COMMANDERS.

GO!

The Washington, D.C. sports scene goes far beyond professional teams. LOCAL COLLEGES such as George Washington, American University and Georgetown University (to name just a few!) provide plenty of top-flight action for sports-crazed fans.

Learn the stories of bold thinkers and
BRAVE ADVENTURERS who have carved
a path through the skies, including
Charles Lindbergh, Amelia Earhart, the
Tuskegee Airmen, Jacqueline "Jackie"
Cochran, Neil Loving, and so many more.

In the 1920s, it was impossible
for a Black woman in the United
States of America to earn a
pilot's license—but "impossible"
didn't stop BESSIE COLEMAN.
Bessie moved to France and got
her license to fly—becoming
the first woman, and the first
African American woman,
to do so!

Marvel at triumphs of the imagination
from the world of SCIENCE FICTION,
including an 11-foot model of the
Starship *Enterprise* from the original
Star Trek television show and the
actual T-70 X-wing Starfighter
from the film *Star Wars: The Rise of
Skywalker*.

The National Air and Space Museum

It is one of the oldest dreams of humankind—to fly like
a bird! The National Air and Space Museum documents
the history of flight, telling us the story of our triumphant
successes and our agonizing failures through thousands of
artifacts, including dangling planes, awe-inspiring rocket
ships, real-life spacesuits, and more. Step inside and we'll
be up, up and away!

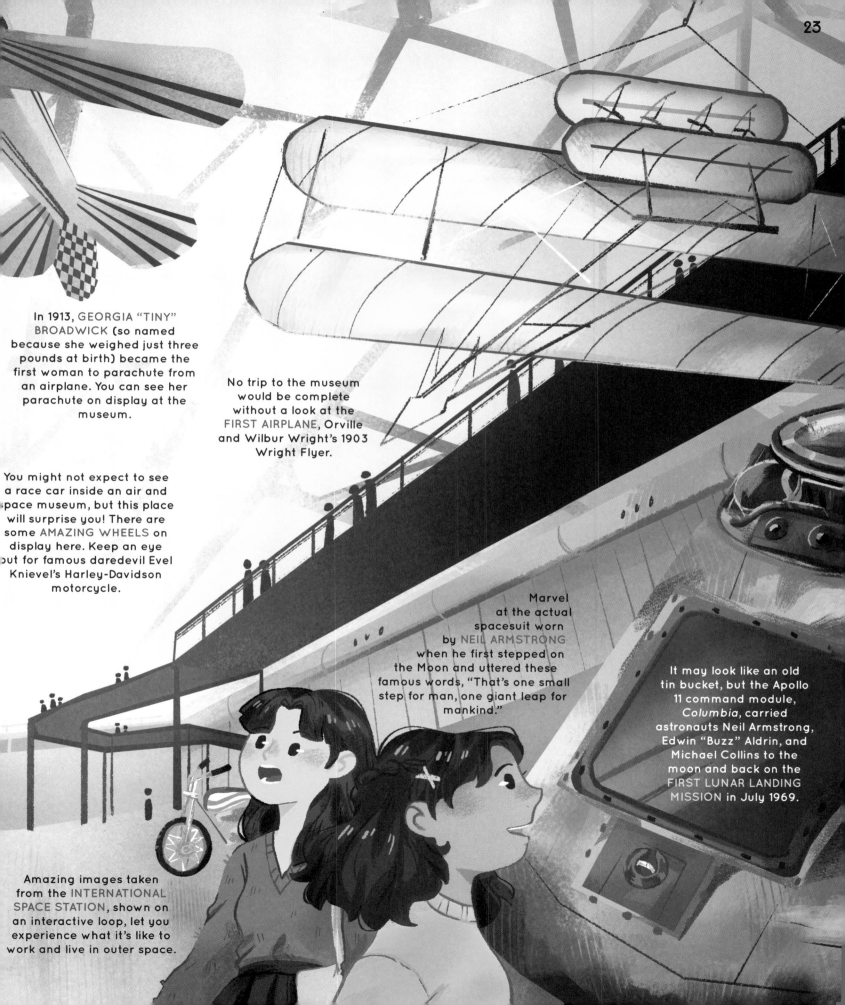

In 1913, GEORGIA "TINY" BROADWICK (so named because she weighed just three pounds at birth) became the first woman to parachute from an airplane. You can see her parachute on display at the museum.

No trip to the museum would be complete without a look at the FIRST AIRPLANE, Orville and Wilbur Wright's 1903 Wright Flyer.

You might not expect to see a race car inside an air and space museum, but this place will surprise you! There are some AMAZING WHEELS on display here. Keep an eye out for famous daredevil Evel Knievel's Harley-Davidson motorcycle.

Marvel at the actual spacesuit worn by NEIL ARMSTRONG when he first stepped on the Moon and uttered these famous words, "That's one small step for man, one giant leap for mankind."

It may look like an old tin bucket, but the Apollo 11 command module, *Columbia*, carried astronauts Neil Armstrong, Edwin "Buzz" Aldrin, and Michael Collins to the moon and back on the FIRST LUNAR LANDING MISSION in July 1969.

Amazing images taken from the INTERNATIONAL SPACE STATION, shown on an interactive loop, let you experience what it's like to work and live in outer space.

With around three in every ten plant species in the U.S. threatened with extinction, the exhibits at the garden explore how humankind can protect and care for RARE AND ENDANGERED PLANTS.

AMERICA'S FOUNDING FATHERS were committed to life, liberty, and the pursuit of gardening! George Washington, Thomas Jefferson, and James Madison all supported the idea of a botanic garden for the study of plants.

The orchids are among the garden's most celebrated collections. There are usually HUNDREDS OF ORCHIDS on display at any time, featuring all manner of colors, shapes, and smells.

You'll feel as though you're walking through a real-life desert as you spot CACTI AND SUCCULENTS from some of the world's most arid environments.

In 2019, the garden added its first GREEN ROOF on the Conservatory, using mostly hardy sedum and native grasses.

The garden showcases a DAZZLING ARRAY OF ROSES. In 1986, President Reagan declared the rose the National Flower of the United States.

Visitors can climb up to a mezzanine level near the top of the greenhouse for a walk through a TROPICAL FOREST TREE CANOPY and a dizzying bird's eye view of the plants 24-feet below!

Behold the CORPSE FLOWER! Why that name? Well, take a whiff! It STINKS and the smell is often compared to that of rotting flesh. The corpse flower blooms for just two or three days of the year.

In the CHILDREN'S GARDEN, kids can jump right into the action—digging in the dirt, using gardening tools, and climbing through a vine tunnel.

The plants aren't just for tourists. The gardens have become a habitat for all sorts of wildlife, and BIRDS are some of the most frequent visitors. To date, more than 130 bird species have been spotted and identified.

The cast iron, 30-foot BARTHOLDI FOUNTAIN was created by Frédéric-Auguste Bartholdi—the designer of the Statue of Liberty! The fountain weighs a whopping 30,440 pounds.

The United States Botanic Garden

The Botanic Garden, located at the foot of the Capitol Building, is an oasis in the busy city. Step inside and you're in a wonderland of sights and smells. Home to a staggering array of native plants, the garden is a place where beauty and conservation come together. You'll see plants of all kinds, from those that can survive in harsh, arid deserts, to those that thrive in lush, tropical forests. In the outdoor gardens, you'll experience a living museum of native plants that changes with the seasons.

Jump into the saddle for a guided HORSE RIDE around a beautiful trail. You won't believe you're still in the heart of the nation's capital city as you trot happily beneath the tree canopy.

Sometimes called "the LUNGS OF THE CITY," the park is home to many types of tree, including oak, cedar, beech, and flowering dogwood.

Even PRESIDENTS need to get away from it all Theodore Roosevelt, a nature enthusiast, used to come to the park to watch birds and Ronald Reagan often rode horses here.

Stare up in wonder at the Rock Creek Park PLANETARIUM, as images of the night sky are projected on the dome-shaped ceiling. Park Rangers give talks about our solar system, the galaxy, and the universe beyond.

Rock Creek Park

Need a break from the bustling city? Rock Creek Park is a favorite getaway for D.C. locals and tourists alike. The park has something for everyone—tennis courts and hiking trails, dense woodlands and waterways, picnic areas, playing fields, rocky outcrops, an amphitheater, and even a planetarium. All of this in an environment where wild animals such as foxes, coyotes, raccoons, beavers, and deer still thrive alongside their human neighbors!

Rock Creek Park is one of the MOST BEAUTIFUL natural city parks in the nation. It's also one of the oldest, having been officially authorized in 1890!

Coming in at twice the size of Central Park in New York City, Rock Creek Park covers a HUGE AREA.

Along Rock Creek Park's 32 MILES OF TRAILS, you'll see people biking, rollerblading, running, and hiking—all enjoying a healthy escape from city life.

The Children's Discovery Room at the Nature Center is a spot for FAMILY FUN—there are games and activities, plus live fish, snakes, turtles, and a busy bee hive.

Rock Creek Park has SPORTS on offer, too! The park features outdoor tennis courts and an 18-hole golf course.

Plant lovers can pick up a map and take a tour of the park's diverse array of NATIVE PLANTS, including American holly, mountain laurel, and jack-in-the-pulpit.

Can't Miss Memorials

There's a lot of ground to cover in Washington, D.C., with dozens of landmarks and attractions to fit in. Here are some of the memorials that are totally worth your time.

The MARTIN LUTHER KING, JR. MEMORIAL pays tribute to the nation's greatest civil rights activist. The design is based on a quote from his famous "I Have a Dream" speech: "Out of the mountain of despair, a stone of hope."

The KOREAN WAR VETERANS MEMORIAL is made up of nineteen statues depicting U.S. soldiers on patrol. An adjacent wall contains more than 2,400 images representing all those who served in Korea.

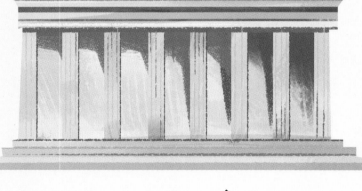

Since its dedication in 1922, the LINCOLN MEMORIAL has become much more than an inspiring tribute to a great leader. The site plays an important role in American life and is a popular destination for marches, rallies, speeches, and peaceful protests.

The WORLD WAR II MEMORIAL honors the more than 400,000 Americans who sacrificed their lives in the conflict between 1939 and 1945. It is one of the most visited attractions on the National Mall.

The ALBERT EINSTEIN MEMORIAL, tucked away in an elm and holly grove, is one of the coolest memorials in the city. The 12-foot-tall bronze figure weighs about 4 tons.

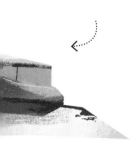

Making up the FRANKLIN DELANO ROOSEVELT MEMORIAL, four outdoor "rooms" tell the story of FDR's four terms in office. A fifth room, called the Prologue Room, features a life-sized FDR sitting in a wheelchair. This statue represents a side of the great leader that he often kept hidden during his lifetime, because of widespread ableism, but is now shown with pride.

A tribute to America's first president, the WASHINGTON MONUMENT is the tallest structure in the city. It took 36 years to build, and if you climb to the top on a clear day, you can see up to 40 miles in every direction.

It is fitting that conservationist and nature-lover THEODORE ROOSEVELT gets his own island and wildlife refuge as his memorial. With nearly two miles of trails through forest and wetlands, the island also features a memorial plaza and 17-foot statue of our most "outdoorsy" president.

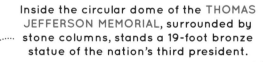

The VIETNAM VETERANS MEMORIAL has become a special place for those who seek to remember lost loved ones. The imposing black granite wall has over 58,000 names carved into its surface.

Inside the circular dome of the THOMAS JEFFERSON MEMORIAL, surrounded by stone columns, stands a 19-foot bronze statue of the nation's third president.

Head to the KEY BRIDGE BOATHOUSE in Georgetown to start your watery adventures on the Potomac River. You can even paddleboard or boat to Theodore Roosevelt Island!

A towpath along the gorgeous CHESAPEAKE AND OHIO CANAL lets you follow the water for a whopping 184.5 miles!

THE YARDS PARK and neighborhood sits beside the Anacostia River. It's a peaceful place for everyone to enjoy, with open grassy areas, a playground, and a riverfront boardwalk to get you closer to the water.

Yikes! Anyone got a sinking feeling? The land and the seawall around the Tidal Basin are actually SLOWLY SINKING. With the basin getting older and sea levels rising due to climate change, the Tidal Basin is now flooding twice a day.

The bridge over the Tidal Basin and the seawall were completed in the 1940s. The engineering firm Alexander & Repass hired both BLACK AND WHITE WORKERS at a time in American history when this practice was still rare.

Are you up for a hike along the river? The CAPITAL CRESCENT TRAIL starts in Georgetown and winds along the Potomac River to Silver Spring, Maryland. The 20-mile Anacostia Riverwalk Trail is also not to be missed.

On the Waterfront

From kayaking to water taxis to paddleboarding, THE WHARF helped establish D.C. as a true waterfront destination. With restaurants, shopping, and spectacular views, its piers and promenades are the perfect spot for riverfront poses, so smile and take a selfie!

It may be true that Washington, D.C. is a long way from the nearest ocean, but never fear, water-lovers, this city still knows how to make a splash! With the Potomac and Anacostia Rivers, new developments at The Wharf and The Yards, and of course old favorites like the Tidal Basin and the Chesapeake and Ohio Canal, there's a wealth of ways for active, adventurous visitors to have fun in and around the water.

The Thomas Jefferson Memorial is considered one of the most beautiful monuments in all of Washington, D.C., thanks in part to its unique location on the TIDAL BASIN. When the weather is clear, the memorial creates a shimmering image on the water.

PADDLE BOATS on the Tidal Basin allow visitors to take in stunning views of the National Mall and, in season, the beauty of the blossoming cherry trees.

With views of the Potomac River and the Key Bridge, GEORGETOWN WATERFRONT PARK offers watery fun for the whole family. Fountains shoot jets of water up into the air, so be prepared to get wet!

Thanks to a very clever feat of engineering, water from the Tidal Basin is used to maintain water levels in the LINCOLN MEMORIAL REFLECTING POOL.

Food, Glorious Food

D.C. is a foodie's paradise, and its most adventurous dishes and delicious flavors reflect the diverse groups of people who've made the District their home. With influences from around the country and around the world, this city has a little bit of everything on the menu!

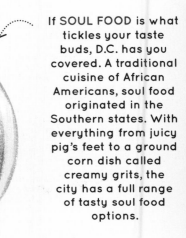

MUMBO SAUCE is a local favorite. Sweet, tangy, and delicious, it's best slathered on chicken wings, but we've even seen it on pizza!

SENATE BEAN SOUP has been on the U.S. Senate dining room menu for more than 100 years! It features navy beans, smoked ham hocks, and onions.

If SOUL FOOD is what tickles your taste buds, D.C. has you covered. A traditional cuisine of African Americans, soul food originated in the Southern states. With everything from juicy pig's feet to a ground corn dish called creamy grits, the city has a full range of tasty soul food options.

With the city being famous for its cherry trees and its annual Cherry Blossom Festival, it's no surprise that the CHERRY is Washington, D.C.'s very own official fruit. Unfortunately, the cherry trees along the Tidal Basin don't actually produce fruit that you can eat!

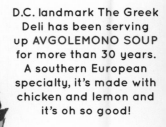

D.C. landmark The Greek Deli has been serving up AVGOLEMONO SOUP for more than 30 years. A southern European specialty, it's made with chicken and lemon and it's oh so good!

Something smells fishy! Since 1805, the MAINE AVENUE FISH MARKET has been serving up seafood to locals and tourists alike. It is the oldest continuously operating fish market in the country!

Check out BLUE CRABS AND OYSTERS from nearby Chesapeake Bay. Order them steamed and spiced, or maybe even baked into a crab cake. That's how you spell Y-U-M!

Summer is all about ice cream. Be on the lookout for SHAVED ICE TREATS and PALETAS, a Mexican spin on the popsicle.

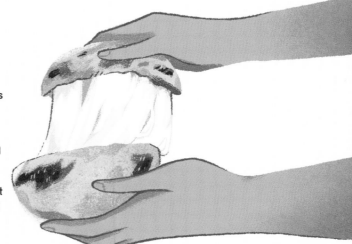

Essentially pancakes made with corn flour and filled with cheese, meat, or beans, SALVADORAN PUPUSAS have become a D.C. staple. They are best served with crunchy curtido cabbage slaw and salsa roja.

D.C. has the largest Ethiopian population outside of Ethiopia, and of course that comes with a wide range of delicious ETHIOPIAN DISHES. Try kitfo, a traditional meal of finely-chopped raw beef mixed with a blend of spices and a butter called niter kibbeh, often served with tangy injera bread.

The ultimate champion of Washington, D.C. street food is the grilled, spicy HALF-SMOKE sausage on a bun. Take a bite and the crisp casing gives a satisfying snap!

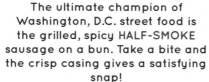

The city has embraced "KFC"— KOREAN FRIED CHICKEN! Eat it plain, spicy hot, or in soy and ginger sauce. You'll find some of the best in the Adams Morgan neighborhood.

The SLAVERY AND FREEDOM exhibit tells the painful history of slavery that is central to the American experience. Visitors can attempt to imagine the lives of individuals damaged by slavery as they view the hymn book of leading abolitionist Harriet Tubman, a Bible owned by Nat Turner (who led a rebellion of enslaved people in 1831), and the sorrowful sight of small shackles made for an enslaved child.

Visitors can reflect while viewing signs from the Jim Crow era of RACIAL SEGREGATION. The signs were used in many public spaces, including restaurants, waiting rooms, and buses, to restrict Black people's freedom. These objects help to open up conversations and provide an opportunity for all Americans to recognize a shared past.

African American contributions to POP CULTURE carve out an important place in the museum. Items include a cape that belonged to soul singer James Brown, musical equipment used by hip-hop producer J Dilla, a chef's jacket worn by the "Queen of Creole Cuisine" Leah Chase, Chuck Berry's apple-red convertible, and a trumpet owned by the legendary musician Louis Armstrong.

The OPRAH WINFREY THEATER, a 350-seat auditorium, offers films, lectures, and other programs for visitors to enjoy and learn from.

The National Museum of African American History and Culture

A one of its kind treasure, this national museum is dedicated to telling the truthful history of African American life and experience. The Museum's expansive collections are organized into three main galleries: History, Culture, and Community. The story it tells is one of resilience, determination, pride, strength, talent, and joy.

The exhibit titled TAKING THE STAGE explores the contributions of African Americans to the stage and screen— celebrating the community's creative achievements and cultural impact.

Paintings, sculptures and other pieces offer insight into how AFRICAN AMERICAN ARTISTS viewed their world and shaped the history of American art.

The museum displays some of the most fabulous work from the trailblazing Black fashion designer ANN LOWE.

"BLACK IS BEAUTIFUL" was a cultural movement of affirmation and self-worth in the 1960s and 1970s. A small but mighty pin bearing these words can be viewed in the museum, documenting that important historical moment.

In 1972, SHIRLEY CHISHOLM became the first Black woman elected to Congress. She later ran for president and tirelessly fought for the rights of marginalized groups. You can see her famous campaign poster in the museum.

ALTHEA GIBSON was the first African American to win a Grand Slam tennis title. The museum is home to some of the rackets and medals that tell her incredible story.

The museum won an architectural award for its ECO-FRIENDLY FEATURES, including rooftop solar panels and a water recycling system that saves an estimated 8 million gallons of water per year.

NBA superstar LeBron James donated $2.5 million to support the museum's exhibit on the accomplishments of boxer MUHAMMAD ALI. You can even see training robes worn by the legend himself.

Cool Neighborhoods

A city is so much more than its buildings, parks, museums, and monuments. It's about the lives of everyday people who make it their home and bring that vital energy to its streets. Step into some of Washington, D.C.'s coolest neighborhoods, each offering a unique slice of life, filled with personality and local culture.

The U STREET CORRIDOR is famed for its food, music, and nightlife. Once known as the District's "Black Broadway," it is a center of African American culture and home to historic institutions such as the Lincoln Theatre. Look out for *Encore*, a sculpture of jazz legend Duke Ellington, outside the Howard Theatre.

Newly revitalized and ultra-cool, H STREET NE has become a one-and-a-half-mile stretch dotted with funky shops and chill cafes. If your feet get tired from all the sightseeing, you can always ride up and down on the D.C. streetcar!

The Shaw neighborhood is one of the city's hippest spots, with BLAGDEN ALLEY being a favorite for snacks, drinks and window-shopping. Even the coolest customers are sure to be impressed by the collection of colorful murals painted across walls and garage doors.

LITTLE ETHIOPIA, located within the Shaw neighborhood, is known for its Ethiopian community, culture and businesses. The many restaurants offer Ethiopian cuisine at its most delicious. Stop for a bite to eat and a traditional Ethiopian coffee ceremony.

You can find some of D.C.'s largest and most beautiful mansions along EMBASSY ROW on Massachusetts Avenue. With over 170 foreign embassies located here, you might even meet a diplomat!

FOGGY BOTTOM got its name because, well, the fog tends to linger here! Its most famous landmark is the John F. Kennedy Center for the Performing Arts, which puts on world-class music, dance, and dramatic performances. Take your seats please!

The ADAMS MORGAN neighborhood may be less than 5 square miles, but this multicultural and lively neighborhood is still a "must" for anyone wishing to see—and taste—D.C. at its most diverse and its most delicious! People from all over the world find a welcome home in Adams Morgan.

When in D.C., do what the Washingtonians do and flock to DUPONT CIRCLE, relax by the fountain, and people-watch! This cosmopolitan neighborhood offers something for everyone, especially on Sundays when locals and visitors can pick up fresh fruit and vegetables at the weekly farmers market.

NEIGHBORHOOD FESTIVALS enliven the city and can be found throughout the year. One of the best is Fiesta Asia!, a Pan-Asian heritage festival that takes over the streets. You'll hear music from different cultures, marvel at the dancers—and you'll surely see a massive, colorful dragon!

In the heart of CHINATOWN, the Friendship Archway (H Street and 7th Street) was built to symbolize the positive relationship between Washington and its sister city, Beijing in China.

The NACOTCHTANK PEOPLE used this area as a trading village in the 1600s. The arrival of European settlers proved disastrous for the Indigenous population. By 1700, many had died from European diseases and the rest had been forcibly driven off their land.

Step back in time and get a taste for old Georgetown by visiting any of the three HISTORIC HOMES that have been converted into museums: Dumbarton Oaks, Dumbarton House, and Tudor Place.

Take a walk along the tow-path of the CHESAPEAKE AND OHIO CANAL, a 184.5-mile dirt and stone path that links Washington, D.C. with the Ohio River Valley.

Who is George, anyway? Good question! George Town, as the area was originally called, was established in 1751, with many people believing it was named after the KING OF ENGLAND, George II, who reigned from 1727 until his death in 1760.

The canal became a NATIONAL PARK in 1971 and is now a peaceful spot to fish, picnic, and take in the sights of the neighborhood.

Don't forget your lifejacket! Visitors can paddle their way down the canal, with KAYAKS AND CANOES available to rent. Go it alone or kick back and enjoy a guided tour.

Historic Georgetown

Sometimes, when we visit a busy city, it can feel overwhelming or even exhausting. One of the best ways to get to know a place is to stop racing around and slow down, and there is no better spot to do this than Georgetown. Wander along a tree-lined street, sipping a refreshing drink and ducking into local shops. Or find a delicious ice cream and eat it as you admire the prettily painted townhouses. Take a moment to explore one of the oldest and most beautiful parts of the city.

Keep your eyes peeled for the OLD STONE HOUSE, the oldest structure (still on its original foundation) in Washington, D.C., built in 1766.

Visitors with a SWEET TOOTH can eat their way through Georgetown, tasting an array of macarons, cupcakes, and other sweets at the many bakeries and patisseries in town.

Georgetown is the site of many COLORFUL MURALS, including a big bike, a famous wave, fantastic flowers and optical illusions. How many can you find?

If you'd like a glimpse of modern college life (without all the homework and tests) visitors are welcome to wander the 104-acre grounds of GEORGETOWN UNIVERSITY. Washington's oldest university, it was founded in 1789.

After the Civil War, students at Georgetown university chose the SCHOOL COLORS (blue and gray), based on the colors of the uniforms of soldiers from the North and the South. This combination represents the unity of all students.

Museums and More Museums

No city does museums better than Washington, D.C. Forget any ideas you might have about dusty, stale places with boring signs, D.C.'s museums are vibrant, exciting, beautiful, fresh, and full of surprises.

For a dazzling range of the best in contemporary art, head to the HIRSHHORN MUSEUM AND SCULPTURE GARDEN. From striking cubist masterpieces and dreamy surrealist artworks, to show-stopping performance and visual media pieces and one of the best sculpture collections in the world, this museum has modern art covered.

The NATIONAL MUSEUM OF THE AMERICAN INDIAN documents and celebrates the living cultures, history, and art of Indigenous peoples throughout the Western Hemisphere. The museum's collections include works of religious and historical importance and a vast photo archive, as well as articles produced for everyday use and research.

The NATIONAL MUSEUM OF AMERICAN HISTORY preserves a record of America's past. Browse the rooms and discover all sorts of American gems, including Dorothy's ruby slippers from the movie *The Wizard of Oz*, Abraham Lincoln's hat, Thomas Jefferson's portable writing desk, Muhammad Ali's boxing gloves, and even Kermit the Frog!

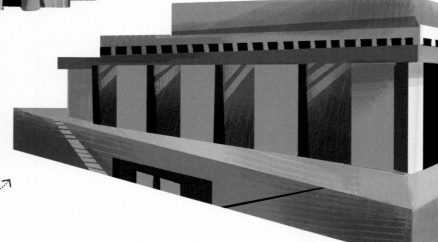

Do you have what it takes to go undercover as a spy? Find out at the INTERNATIONAL SPY MUSEUM. Highlights include a pistol disguised as a lipstick, a wristwatch camera, a code-breaking machine, and a James Bond car. The museum also has digital interactives throughout, where you can complete spy-challenges like remembering your cover identity and cracking secret codes.

Born into slavery, Frederick Douglass became a leading visionary in the anti-slavery, abolitionist movement. Cedar Hill, the house where he lived his last 17 years, is now open as the FREDERICK DOUGLASS NATIONAL HISTORIC SITE. Visitors can see "the growlery," a tiny stone cabin where Douglass went to read, write, and think.

Ready for something different? The NATIONAL BONSAI AND PENJING MUSEUM is home to more than 100 miniature trees and shrubs. Originating from Japan, China, and North America, these miniature masterpieces are carefully tended by the museum's skilled staff—all in a soothing, reflective environment that's off the beaten path.

For anyone who loves reading, the LIBRARY OF CONGRESS is a must-see. You are welcome to walk the floor of the magnificent Grand Reading Room, with its stained-glass skylights, marbled floors, and gorgeous murals. The largest library in the world, this collection is home to tens of millions of books, so take your pick!

The National Zoo

The National Zoo is a top stop for nature enthusiasts young and old. The zoo is home to a diverse range of more than 2,500 animals from around the world. From great apes, big cats, and two-toed sloths, to monkeys, meerkats, and mangrove snakes, you'll be able to spot them all at Washington D.C.'s wildest attraction!

GIANT PANDAS have long been the star attraction at the zoo. The zoo's first two pandas—– were gifted to the American people by Chinese Premier Zhou Enlai following a historic visit from President Nixon in 1972.

Each panda can eat up to 100 POUNDS OF BAMBOO every day! Their diet is supplemented with biscuits, carrots, sweet potatoes, and apples.

Join the zoo's herd of ASIAN ELEPHANTS and experience the sights, the sounds, and, yes, even the smells of these beautiful, and incredibly intelligent, creatures.

The AMERICAN TRAIL introduces you to creatures native to the U.S. and Canada. Keep an eye out for local legends, including California sea lions, gray seals, beavers, otters, eagles, and wolves.

From coral conservation and elephant-tracking, to restoring and preserving the prairies, teams of environmentalists and scientists from the zoo work hard to SAVE SPECIES AND HABITATS around the world.

The zoo is home to Bornean orangutans, western lowland gorillas, howler monkeys, and many more of our PRIMATE RELATIONS. Several of the zoo's orangutans take part in a computer-based language project where scientists study how they think.

Trek through a lush jungle in the Amazonia exhibit, a vibrant ecosystem replicating the AMAZON RAINFOREST, with more than 350 plant species and countless fascinating creatures to spot, including two-toed sloths, red-bellied piranhas, roseate spoonbills, and electric eels.

A wide range of AMPHIBIANS AND REPTILES are housed in the indoor exhibits. The reptiles often use camouflage to hide, and can be very good at it! But don't worry, keen-eyed volunteers are stationed nearby to point them out.

While petting the big cats is probably a no-no, you can get up close and personal with some of the friendlier animals at the KIDS' FARM. You'll meet alpacas, chickens, goats, cows, and miniature donkeys.

The keepers at the zoo work very hard to make sure the animals are HAPPY AND HEALTHY— and that includes regular checkups and weigh-ins. Hop up onto those scales now, crocodile!

Big animals often get the most attention, but you'll love the SMALL MAMMAL HOUSE. Where else could you watch a naked mole rat tunneling underground, or spot tiny golden lion tamarins scampering through the branches?

Fun Festivals

Washington, D.C. is bursting with festivals. No matter what time of year, there's fun to be found in this city that knows how to party! From blasting music, extravagant parades, and spectacular fireworks, to celebrations of books, bikes, and barbecues, there's something for everyone.

PASSPORT DC is a month-long festival in May. In tribute to Washington D.C.'s international culture, foreign embassies along Embassy Row open their doors, offering food, art, and dance from around the world.

If it's summer in the city, it's time for DC JAZZFEST. The event offers a diverse selection of jazz artists performing in a variety of venues throughout the city. Many shows are free!

There's nothing like the SMITHSONIAN FOLKLIFE FESTIVAL for a sprawling, music-filled, family-friendly day on the National Mall. Even Abe Lincoln will be there, listening from his marble chair.

The NATIONAL CHERRY BLOSSOM FESTIVAL is one of the most anticipated events of the year. It marks the end of winter and celebrates the donation of 3,020 gorgeous cherry trees from the Mayor of Tokyo in 1912.

Make sure to check out the annual KITE FESTIVAL. It includes a competition, demonstrations, and even a chance to build your own kite. Up, up, and away!

EMANCIPATION DAY takes place every April 16. A parade, concert, and fireworks honor the day when President Lincoln signed the Compensated Emancipation Act of 1862, freeing over 3,000 enslaved persons in the District of Columbia.

There's nothing better than a good book! That is unless it's the NATIONAL BOOK FESTIVAL hosted by the Library of Congress.

Every June, residents and visitors gather to celebrate LGBTQ+ communities at PRIDE. With a parade, a concert, and tasty food stalls, it's a colorful celebration of love, diversity, and inclusion.

Grab your helmet and hop on a bike for the annual DC BIKE RIDE. The 20-mile route takes you past all the best sights of the city.

VROOM, VROOM! Check out some cool wheels at the WASHINGTON AUTO SHOW, the city's largest annual indoor event.

D.C. is having a block party and you're invited! The high-energy H STREET FESTIVAL includes live bands, artists, and a mouth-watering array of different foods.

Celebrate the FOURTH OF JULY with a concert on the Mall and a thrilling fireworks display. Where better to celebrate the nation's birthday?

Hungry? Come on over to the BARBECUE BATTLE, where the country's best "pitmasters" deliver cooking demos and fantastic flavors.

The magnificent circular room on the second floor is called the ROTUNDA. It is here that the nation pays tribute to its most important people when they pass away, a tradition called "lying in state" for government officials or military officers, and "lying in honor" for private citizens.

The Rotunda is home to 100 STATUES of important citizens in US history, two per state. Many other paintings and statues appear throughout the rest of the building.

When civil rights activist ROSA PARKS died in 2005, she lay in honor in the Rotunda. Recognized for her commitment to freedom and equality, she was the first woman and only the second African American to receive this honor.

THIRTEEN WOMEN are currently represented in the National Statuary Hall Collection, including the pilot Amelia Earhart (Kansas), the guide, interpreter and explorer Sakakawea (North Dakota), and the author and disability activist Helen Keller (Alabama).

The statue that stands on the top of the Capitol Dome is called the STATUE OF FREEDOM. Although it looks teeny tiny from the ground, it's actually 19 feet tall and weighs around 15,000 pounds!

The Capitol has approximately 540 rooms and MORE THAN 650 WINDOWS (108 of which are found in the dome!).

The U.S. Capitol

In the words of Abraham Lincoln, democracy means a government "of the people, for the people, by the people," and there is no building in America more symbolic of those ideals than the United States Capitol Building. It is home to the nation's legislative branch of government, meaning it's where the country's laws are made. The Senate meets in the north wing and the House of Representatives meets in the south wing. Capped by an iconic white dome, you can see the Capitol from the National Mall or, if you are lucky, on the reverse side of a $50 bill!

CONGRESS first met in the Capitol Building on November 17, 1800.

The Capitol has been changed and expanded many times over the years. The original building was designed by WILLIAM THORNTON, a doctor who had no formal training in architecture!

The Capitol stands within a large park originally designed by landscape architect Frederick Law Olmsted. The 274-acre grounds feature a collection of more than 4,800 TREES.

Shhh, don't tell anyone: the Capitol has miles of SECRET UNDERGROUND TUNNELS. For the use of senators and members of the House, they are never seen by visitors.

There is an EMPTY CRYPT under the Capitol that was supposed to be the burial place of George Washington. Instead, he wished for his remains to be buried at his home in Mount Vernon, Virginia.

Change Makers

Countless creative and courageous Washingtonians have made their mark on the world around us. Here, meet just a handful of the District's influential thinkers, trailblazers, writers, activists, athletes, and leaders. Many of these go-getters were the first from their community to achieve a goal, effect change, or do something super cool.

Author of more than 100 books for young people, JEAN CRAIGHEAD GEORGE grew up in Washington, D.C. A love of nature has always been central to her work and she's written many classics, including *Julie of the Wolves* and *My Side of the Mountain*.

"The Science Guy," BILL NYE grew up in the D.C. area and went on to become one of the most popular and influential scientists of our time, thanks to his many appearances on television and elsewhere.

Called "the man with a thousand moves," ELGIN BAYLOR was an unstoppable force in the National Basketball Association, bringing a brand of bouncy athleticism that the sport had not seen before. He was an eleven-time All-Star and his above-the-rim style paved the way for modern star of the game.

Born in Washington, D.C., TV comedian and talk show host STEPHEN COLBERT spent his early years in nearby Bethesda, Maryland. Fun fact: he teamed up with Ben & Jerry's to create the fudge-and-caramel swirled "Americone Dream" flavor!

Dancer, singer, and actress CHITA RIVERA was born in Washington, D.C. under the name Dolores Conchita Figueroa del Rivero. She is best known for her energetic performance as Anita in the Broadway musical *West Side Story*.

MARIAN ANDERSON was an inspirational African American singer. In 1939, in a stand against racial prejudice that had prohibited her from performing in certain venues, Marian was invited to the steps of the Lincoln Memorial where she delivered a free concert to a crowd of tens of thousands of people of all races. Her brave and moving performance became a hugely symbolic moment for the country.

AL GORE grew up a Senator's son, living at the Fairfax Hotel on Embassy Row. The nation's 45th vice president, he was awarded the Nobel Prize in 2007 for his efforts to raise awareness about climate change.

At just 15 years old, KATIE LEDECKY made a big splash! She won her first gold medal at the 2012 Olympics in the 800m freestyle. She's won nine Olympic gold medals and twenty-one World Championship titles so far—the most of any female swimmer in history.

A mathematician, astronomer, author, and inventor, BENJAMIN BANNEKER was considered the first African American "man of science." He was appointed by President George Washington to work as a surveyor, helping to design the blueprints for Washington, D.C. itself!

The legendary soul singer MARVIN GAYE grew up in various housing projects in Washington, D.C. Learning to sing in church and as part of the Randall Junior High Glee Club, he went on to become a worldwide sensation. His hits include "I Heard It Through the Grapevine" and "What's Going On."

BILL WATTERSON is known (and loved) for his wildly popular comic strip about a boy and his imaginary friend, *Calvin and Hobbes*. Watterson ended the strip in 1995 with Calvin telling his friend, "It's a magical world, Hobbes, ol' buddy. Let's go exploring."

The DC JAZZFEST has become an annual highlight, bringing a talent-filled lineup to the city at the end of each summer. Performances take place at dozens of venues, including free outdoor shows at The Wharf, D.C.'s coolest waterfront neighborhood.

A proud native of the city, and a twelve-time Grammy nominee, MESHELL NDEGEOCELLO blends jazz, funk, reggae, and hip-hop into her skillful sound.

If D.C. has a specific sound, it has to be GO-GO MUSIC. Inspired by blues, soul, and salsa, this homegrown music is a subgenre of funk and is famous for its deep grooves, heavy percussion, and use of "call-and-response" between a vocalist and the crowd.

No matter what day of the week, there's always LIVE MUSIC somewhere in Washington, D.C. The District's best and most popular venues include The Anthem, 9:30 Club, Union Stage, Black Cat, DC9, and Echostage.

One of the earliest major musical figures from Washington, D.C. was composer JOHN PHILIP SOUSA. Born in 1854, he wrote "Stars and Stripes Forever," the most beloved march in American history.

The jazz legend DUKE ELLINGTON is one of D.C.'s proudest sons. He began playing piano at just seven years old. When he died at the age of 75, his last words were, "Music is how I live, why I live, and how I will be remembered."

Washington, D.C. is home to a growing Latin population, enriching the city not only with their cultures and delicious food, but also with their music! Look out for the DISTRITO MUSIC FEST, featuring a range of acts in celebration of Latin heritage.

The D.C. Music Scene

Does D.C. dig music? You better believe it! When the music's playing, the streets come alive. From funk and jazz to punk, indie rock, and of course the city's beloved "go-go" music, Washington, D.C. has something for every musical taste. So what are you waiting for? Pump up the volume and let's dance in D.C.!

The John F. Kennedy Center for the PERFORMING ARTS is renowned for showcasing the world's finest performers. Each year the prestigious Kennedy Center Honors recognize a select few artists who have contributed greatly to cultural life in the U.S., including musicians of all kinds.

Co-founded by D.C.-native Ian MacKaye, the independent record label DISCHORD RECORDS helped earn the city a reputation for hardcore punk and indie rock.

CHUCK BROWN, the legendary leader of the band The Soul Searchers, is known as "the Godfather of Go-Go." He was the driving force behind the genre when it developed in the 1970s.

Those Wild and Wacky Presidents

History has taught us many important facts about different "Commanders in Chief" through the years. But each of those serious, busy presidents is hiding a unique, and sometimes quirky, personality. Read on and you'll see!

At a White House reception on January 1, 1907, TEDDY ROOSEVELT (president number 26) set a world record for the most handshakes in a day, with an incredible 8,513!

BENJAMIN HARRISON (president number 23) refused to touch the light switches in the White House. The year was 1891 and electricity was a brand new phenomenon, so he was terrified of being electrocuted!

It's a tie for tallest president between ABRAHAM LINCOLN (president number 16) and LYNDON JOHNSON (president number 36). They were both around 6'4".

JAMES GARFIELD (president number 20) was the first left-handed president.

JOHN ADAMS (president number 2) and his wife, Abigail, were prolific pen-pals, exchanging more than 1,000 letters during their lifetimes!

RUTHERFORD B. HAYES (president number 19) had the first telephone installed in the White House. The number was easy to remember: 1.

Who was the first president to visit all 50 states while in office? Don't guess George Washington (president number 1), because there were only thirteen states when he took office in 1789! The correct answer? RICHARD NIXON (president number 37).

Four years before becoming president, JIMMY CARTER (president number 39) filed a report to say that he'd seen a UFO!

GEORGE H. W. BUSH (president number 41) really didn't like broccoli. In fact, he banned it from being served on the presidential airplane, Air Force One.

Believe it or not, Allan Hoover, the son of HERBERT HOOVER (president number 31), had two pet alligators that lived in their bathtub, but often escaped. Snap, snap!

JAMES POLK (president number 11) banned dancing and card playing inside the White House. Other than that, he was a fun guy!

The "CRACKED-PLATE" PORTRAIT of Abraham Lincoln, created by Alexander Gardner, is one of the most valuable photographs in American history. The image conveys his deep weariness at the end of the Civil War. During the reproduction process, a crack appeared in the glass-plate negative so Gardner made only a single print before throwing away the damaged plate.

The Gallery boasts a selection of world-famous portraits showing great American historical figures. The centerpiece of the Hall of Presidents is the classic LANSDOWNE PORTRAIT of George Washington.

Born into slavery, HARRIET TUBMAN escaped to Philadelphia and later served as a "conductor" on the Underground Railroad, leading countless enslaved people to freedom. The gallery holds photographs of this inspirational abolitionist and social activist.

In the past, PRESIDENTIAL PORTRAITS were often serious, formal and even a little stuffy. But many contemporary artists have explored new and unusual ways of portraying presidents and first ladies. Don't miss President Obama's leafy background, or the super cool portraits of Jacqueline Kennedy and Michelle Obama.

In addition to its vast collection of presidential portraits, the museum is home to an incredible range of WELL-KNOWN FACES, including Charlie Chaplin, Sequoyah, Venus and Serena Williams, Muhammad Ali, Dr. Anthony Fauci, Ava DuVernay, Hank Aaron, Henrietta Lacks, Maya Lin, Pocahontas (whose real name was Matoaka), Alexander Hamilton, and many more.

National Portrait Gallery

Every museum and gallery tells a story. Some do it with fossils and skeletons, some do it with sculptures or ancient artifacts, and some even do it with postage stamps. Washington, D.C.'s National Portrait Gallery is no exception—it tells the story of America through paintings and photographs of people. The Gallery houses pictures of actors and activists, presidents and poets, and many others who have had a hand in shaping history.

A Girl Scout might enjoy the beautiful portrait of JULIETTE GORDON LOW, founder of the Girl Scouts in the U.S. in 1912. Low's dream was for every girl to embrace their strengths, get outdoors, and find ways to make the world a better place.

Spot legendary Mexican artist FRIDA KAHLO, captured in all her glory by artist Magda Pach.

In 1996, the National Portrait Gallery purchased the earliest known daguerreotype (an early photograph) of abolitionist JOHN BROWN. The portrait was taken by photographer Augustus Washington and it sold for $115,000.

Stop, THIEF! On New Year's Eve, 1984, there was a serious theft at the museum—but it wasn't a portrait that was stolen. Instead, a robber broke into a display case and took four valuable documents, written and signed by Abraham Lincoln, Ulysses S. Grant, George Meade, and George Armstrong Custer. But don't panic, the FBI recovered the documents and they were safely returned.

Weird, Weirder, Weirdest

Washington, D.C. can get weird when it wants to. Sometimes the best things in life don't fit neatly into any one category, but that's kind of the definition of quirky, isn't it? Here is a collection of the odd, the uncanny, and the downright weird—enjoy!

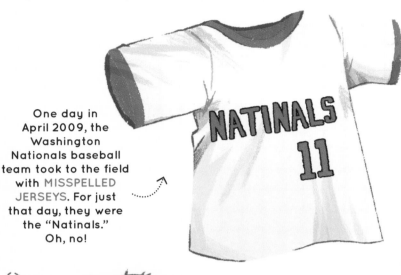

One day in April 2009, the Washington Nationals baseball team took to the field with MISSPELLED JERSEYS. For just that day, they were the "Natinals." Oh, no!

In 1814, invading British troops tried to burn the city to the ground, but a FREAK STORM, possibly a hurricane, arrived just in time to extinguish hundreds of fires. Washington, D.C. was saved!

A RED PANDA named Rusty once escaped from the city zoo. But don't panic, he was found the next day up a tree enjoying the sights of the Adams Morgan neighborhood.

Pass the popcorn! During his four-year term, President Jimmy Carter watched an estimated 480 MOVIES in the White House movie theater.

Among the many gargoyles that decorate the National Cathedral, you can find DARTH VADER!

In the National Museum of Health and Medicine, there's a display of BONE FRAGMENTS and hair from President Lincoln's skull, sitting right beside the bullet that killed him. Gruesome!

Nobody likes a smelly senator! Which is exactly why they installed MARBLE BATHTUBS in the Capitol Building in 1859.

Since its big beginnings, Washington, D.C. has SHRUNK! George Washington originally chose 100 square miles of land in Maryland and Virginia for the site of the nation's capital. However, 31 square miles were returned to Virginia in 1847, leaving today's D.C. smaller, but just as mighty.

A good listener can tell when the presidential motorcade is coming. The SIRENS from these special cars have a different tone than ordinary police car sirens.

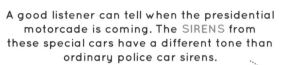

D.C. has its own BARBIE POND— a famous spot where anonymous artists create funny, light-hearted displays featuring Barbie and other dolls for passing tourists and residents to enjoy.

Presidents and their families often have animals living in the White House—and not just dogs and cats. PRESIDENTIAL PETS have included a bear, a lizard, a pig, a badger, a macaw, a snake, a one-legged rooster, sheep, a hyena, a barn owl, a pony, a bobcat, a wallaby, lion cubs, and a pygmy hippo!

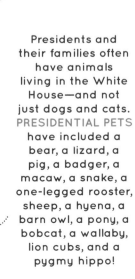

Whoops! Washington is MISSING A STREET! There are lettered streets throughout the city—but there's no J. That's weird!

Index

0-9

A

B

C

D

Major League Professional Sports Teams

National Football League
Washington Commanders
Major League Baseball
Washington Nationals
National Basketball Association
Washington Wizards
Women's National Basketball Association
Washington Mystics
Major League Soccer
D.C. United
National Women's Soccer League
Washington Spirit
National Hockey League
Washington Capitals